Poetry In Motion

A Collection of Poetry, Rhyme & Song

Vol. 1

Neal Sellers

POETRY IN MOTION
A COLLECTION OF POETRY, RHYME & SONG

First Edition Published 2024

Copyright © Neal Sellers 2023

The right of Neal Sellers to be identified as the Author of the Work has been asserted by him in accordance with the Copyright, Designs, and Patents Act 1988.

All rights reserved. No part of this publication may be reproduced or transmitted in any form or by any means without prior permission of the Copyright owner. Any person who does any unauthorized act in relation to this publication may be liable to criminal prosecution and civil claims for damages.

This anthology is a work of fiction. All characters, names, locations, situations, and events are either products of the author's imagination or used fictitiously. Any resemblance to any person, place, or event is purely coincidental.

POETRY IN MOTION
A COLLECTION OF POETRY, RHYME & SONG

Cover Design by Charlyn Samson
Color Photo by Malachi Somerville

Poetry, Rhyme & Song
From the 80's, 90's & 2000's

Dedicated to Creative Spirits in every genre...

And to my mother, Lethia B. Sellers,
who nourished my creative curiosities...
Continued R.I.P.

Table of Contents - Vol. 1

Poem	Title	Page
No. 1	Some Thoughts From The Vault	39
No. 2	Don't Mind Me	11
No. 3	This Place I Know	163
No. 4	The Sands Of Time	125
No. 5	A Sweet View Of Reality	153
No. 6	A Taste For Sweetness	83
No. 7	A Diamond Reborn	119
No. 8	Sonnie Days	105
No. 9	China Doll	75
No. 10	We	143
No. 11	Live Your Life	21
No. 12	Community Activist	91
No. 13	Gambling On Survival	133
No. 14	My Greatest Achievement	1
No. 15	The Nature Of Humanity	65
No. 16	Plight Of A Writer	99
No. 17	The Crux Of The Matter	31
No. 18	Sea Of Chaff	47
No. 19	The Growth Of Thought	57
No. 20	Bliss	113
No. 21	Depth Of Perception	61
No. 22	Mesmerized	25
No. 23	The Sand Of The Seas	167
No. 24	One Ticket, Please	15
No. 25	Seduction	137
No. 26	The Favorite Girls	173
No. 27	Tranquility	35
No. 28	Who Wants To Be King?	157
No. 29	Nature's Nemesis	51

No. 30	Life Finds A Way	77
No. 31	Night Owl	95
No. 32	Seed Of Destruction	85
No. 33	Hear Ye... Hear Ye	43
No. 34	Half Man... Half Amazing	103
No. 35	She Be The Baddest...	69
No. 36	Pit Bull In A Skirt	147
No. 37	Blind Intentions	5
No. 38	God Almighty	107
No. 39	The Guise Of The Night	129
No. 40	Rejuvenating	115
No. 41	Primitive Understandings	123

Rhyme Title	Page
...And You Don't Stop	49
Clap Clap Clap	165
Favorite Girls	3
Feel The Heat/Brooklyn Freestyle	101
Girls Of Today	127
Life Of A Playboy	67
Light... Life... & Love	13
Nadia	155
Poetry In Motion (The Gift Of Gab)	93
Rhymin' The Blues	135
Soul To Body	117
Street Life Freestyle	145
The Rabbit Hole	23
Verbal Gymnastics	41
We Came Here To Party (That's What's Up) Freestyle	59
Young... Gifted... & Wack!	33

Song Title	Page
2 Smooth (Blues)	159
Bedroom Eyes	27
Capture The Rhythm	87
Don't Take It Away	139
Dreams To Be Reality	7
Fire	45
Forever And A Day	131
I Just Want To Be Your Friend	63
I Live For You	17
Knock, Knock... It's Love	149
Make Me Love You Again	71
Party People	109
The Insanity That We Call Love	79
We Came Here To Party (That's What's Up)	97
Which Way Is Up?	37
You Better Love Me	121
You Got To Go	53
You'll Never Walk Alone	169

NOTES/THOUGHTS

MY GREATEST ACHIEVEMENT
(LESLIE SELLERS)

NEAL SELLERS
3/8/23
7:32 a.m.

You are my destiny, you are my remain
You are the cure within my life of bitterness, sorrow and pain
Confirmation came as you stood in Niagara rain
You are the sanctuary I shall not refrain
In a world of disdain, you deserve nothing less
Than a love forever that I pray God continues to bless
I've accomplished many things but I must publicly confess
My greatest achievement was getting you to say "Yes."

NOTES/THOUGHTS

FAVORITE GIRLS

...Known to the world as my favorite girls, Joie Tiyler and Charli Camryn
Number one with a bullet on the Pop charts. Get it?
From the start a self-admitted sucker for my heart
The "I love you Daddy's", the Kool Aid smiles
Heed the jokes about them growing up and dating from Frat
I'd simulate cocking the 12 gauge and quip, "Ha! Good luck with that!"
The joy they brought to my life, it can't be quantified, it can't be measured
It can only be treasured
From the house in Shohola to the Honeycomb Hideout to the pizza at Di Fara's on Ave. J
The margherita pizza we'd have at Graziella's
And then there's Candy's, the last pizzeria in Jersey right before the bridge to PA
Instilled integrity and honesty, family was unshakable
And the bond between sisters, it should always be unbreakable
All of this I backed up with this one simple proof
They'd never get in trouble when they told me the truth
The Favorite Girls, the apples of my eye
The reason I traveled six hours to spend 30 secs on surprise
Just so I could stay relevant and be a presence in their lives...

NOTES/THOUGHTS

BLIND INTENTIONS
(Senryu)

NEAL SELLERS
8/31/23
9:09 a.m.

you look right through me
yet i hope with foolish pride
infatuated

NOTES/THOUGHTS

DREAMS TO BE REALITY

Now I lay me down to sleep
I close my eyes and think
About the girl I'd love to meet
I'd know her favorite drink
I'd even know her size of feet
I'd even know her pain
There's nothing that I'd rather gain
Than to know my dreamboat's name

I'd give her love and all my best
A Queen couldn't feel this royal
Her flowers would feel tenderness
I'd plant my seed in her rich soil
I'm searching and I've yet to find
A girl who's only mine
My dreams tell me I'll see some signs
But reality's not kind

Chorus: Why do dreams come true in your mind but not in time?
We seek and search for a love we never seem to find
And then one day that love is found and dreams come true
But now you have no clue why this person's not for you
And still you long for dreams to be reality (4x)
In your heart

NOTES/THOUGHTS

Now every time I dream I cry
And ask myself why... why?
Can't I have peace and happiness?
I don't think I deserve much less
Let me find her and I swear I'll be
The best that I can be
And honey just you wait and see
How this dream becomes reality

Chorus: Why do dreams come true in your mind but not in time?
We seek and search for a love we never seem to find
And then one day that love is found and dreams come true
But now you have no clue why this person's not for you
And still you long for dreams to be reality (4x)

Bridge: Dreams are fairy tales come true and now they haunt you
Eternal flames are lit by hope and now they die too
Trade winds blow inside your mind yet you don't feel them
The fruit in paradise is deadly but you need it

Finale: Because you long for dreams to be reality
And still you long for dreams to be reality
(2x)
In your heart

NOTES/THOUGHTS

DON'T MIND ME

NEAL SELLERS
2/16/92
1:45 p.m.

What does it take to reach the mind?
The sound of a voice or a non-verbal sign?
How can I reach you my brother of mine?
When you can't even read between rhetoric and lines
How can I reach you my sister of mine?
When the feelings you seek I speak... yet I'm weak?
Why do I bother to take the time
To help that brother and sister of mine?
When tunnels are dark... why do I shed light?
When most go left... why do I go right?
When a friend in need takes a friend indeed
Why do I always feel like the friend who bleeds?
When I am strong... the lions roar
If I get weak... those same are no more
Life is such that I handle the rain
'Though its stinging droplets have caused my pain
And as you read the blood of my disdain
I have now drawn strength to cleanse my stain

NOTES/THOUGHTS

LIGHT... LIFE... & LOVE

...Split the world in half, it's now symmetrical
When we examine the halves, they're not identical
Good & Evil, Night & Day, Black and White, Dude, comprende?
Race relations, inflation, deprivation just seem to glide
And don't forget freedom, equality, enterprise on the side
And when it comes to South Africa, USA just seems to hide
And the President on aid to the Homeless, "Psych, I lied!"
What is the issue? Does it affect you?
Que, do they need more light?
Yeah, I think they do!
Twinkle, twinkle, we can go far
The magnitude of brightness depends on the type of star
Some are white dwarfs, some are red giants
Some die violent, but most are just silent
Light... How can I express it more clearly?
A blind man sees in the dark, but not really
Think about it, get the frown off your face
A mind is a terrible thing for you to waste
The sky is the limit, but the limit's not the sky
Reach for the stars, grab yours, then fly
To your aspirations, they're well within sight
Your mind is the key, follow it to the light...

NOTES/THOUGHTS

ONE TICKET, PLEASE
(Haiku)

NEAL SELLERS
7/28/23
12:41 p.m.

listen to the birds
a symphonic melody
for your ears only

NOTES/THOUGHTS

I LIVE FOR YOU

As I look around... I can see the traces of tears upon their faces
And without a sound... I keep screaming for you
Now I lay me down... and the memories surround me
Without you my life cast a void

Take another step... but everywhere I run to I'm still a step from you
I can feel your smile... I can feel your warm embrace
And these tears I cry are bittersweet beyond redemption
Cause I know your pain is gone

Chorus: (So now) I live for you... I live for you
My darling... darling I live for you (2x)

Take another trip... but memories are painful, I see you as my Angel
Guard me as I sway... to and fro throughout the day
Where to begin? Our dreams make up this sentence
So here's a tear for the end of this word (Teardrop)

Chorus: (That's why) I live for you... I live for you
My darling... darling I live for you (2x)

Bridge: I just wish you (3x)
I wish you were here... now
Makin' me laugh the way you used to
Makin' me smile when I refused to
Disrupting my life the way you used to
Just because you knew you could

Raisin' my spirits when I was true blue
Wakin' me up when I declined to
Sharing my life the way it used to...
Used to be... the way it ... used... to... be

Chorus: I live for you... I live for you
My darling... darling I live for you (2x)

NOTES/THOUGHTS

Here we go again... I start to dial your number but you are here no longer
But I see you here... there... everywhere I go
So I promise you that our dreams will not go under
As long as I'm here on this earth

Finale: (Because) I live for you... I live for you
My darling baby... I live for you

NOTES/THOUGHTS

LIVE YOUR LIFE

NEAL SELLERS
7/14/10
12:12 p.m.

Life is an interesting journey
You never know where it will take you
Peaks and valleys, twists and turns, you can get the surprise of your life
Sometimes on the way to where you're going
You might think it's the worst time in your life
But you know what?
At the end of the road
Through all the adversity
If you can get where you wanted to be?
Remember, whatever don't kill ya, makes you stronger...
So live your life

NOTES/THOUGHTS

THE RABBIT HOLE

...The rabbit hole, way down I go
I hear the cackling of the crow, even way down below
And although I'm not DOA today ... maybe tomorrow
I know my time is borrowed
And I swear when I hit my number, me and senorita
Will spend the rest of my days sipping sangria in Navarro
Is the risk worth the end game?
It better be, cause I'm not doing this for the fame, just the fortune
Telling isn't it? Judge me not, lest ye be judged
Plus you have the option whether you choose to indulge
Don't give me the morality, I've already prayed to God and asked for his charity
If that's not how God works, then I'ma need more clarity...

NOTES/THOUGHTS

MESMERIZED
(Senryu)

NEAL SELLERS
7/27/23
8:24 a.m.

caught up in your web
a transic state of prison
escape is futile

NOTES/THOUGHTS

BEDROOM EYES

    Chorus: You don't have to try
            To seduce me with those eyes
            If looks could kill I'd die
            Just close those bedroom eyes

At first glance I noticed those eyes
You didn't seem to mind when you caught me staring
I shook it off cause ya probably been told
A thousand times or more that your eyes are golden
Hypnotic yet exotic yes it's easy to see
You didn't say a word yet your eyes observed me
The venom of a cobra's like the look in your eyes
Innocent but deadly yet ya don't realize... or do you?

    Chorus: You don't have to try
            To seduce me with those eyes
            If looks could kill I'd die
            Just close those bedroom eyes

Your eyes gleam and all I feel is fire
Or maybe I'm mistaken cause your eyes speak desire
I look back and now I see the disguise
The fire and desire's the reflection of my own eyes
Serious mysterious a story unfolds
The eyes are the window to the soul I'm told
Scandalous n' sexy I just cannot be sold
That you don't even understand the power you hold... or do you?

    Chorus: You don't have to try
            To seduce me with those eyes
            If looks could kill I'd die
            Just close those bedroom eyes

NOTES/THOUGHTS

Bridge: Your eyes speak words without saying a word to me (2x)
Look in my eyes tell me what do you see?
If you see what I see it's destined to be
Your eyes lock your soul so just give me the key
So I can unlock you and you can be free

Finale: Don't close those bedroom eyes now

NOTES/THOUGHTS

THE CRUX OF THE MATTER

NEAL SELLERS
3/15/23
12.23 a.m.

Like a volcano erupting, the ideas overflow
The excitement intoxicating
The aftermath is written below
You hear rhyme, I hear no reason
You hibernate during winter, I'm here for every season
You hear the wind howling, I hear a melody for song
You catch my drift, but I'm already gone
Check my adlib
In silence there is noise
In chaos there is beauty
In God there is love
To each other, there lies our duty...

NOTES/THOUGHTS

YOUNG... GIFTED... & WACK!

Let me tell you one thing about the facts of life
A couple hours of pleasure and ya think ya done right
You didn't use no condom cause you thought it was a joke
The girl was so hot, you came in a stroke
You took it as a game, and you laughed for a while
Few months later she was having your child
So to save yourself from all this distortion
You told her right quick to have an abortion
She looked you up and down and said,
"No, no pretty boy, I'm gonna have this sweet cute bundle of joy!"
So she took you home to her Moms n' her Pops
But he was 6'7" and built like a rock
Had muscles of iron and made of steel
And the way he looked at you, he must've knew the deal
That look in his eyes, disgust on his face
Had that feeling, better leave this place
So you ran on home, hurt and shame
Wondering to yourself, "Was it worth the gain?"
But to top it all off, you had a sore and an itch
That girl just gave you syphilis!!!...

NOTES/THOUGHTS

TRANQUILITY
(Haiku)

NEAL SELLERS
7/31/23
2:37 p.m.

the water ripples
see the reflection of self
a sea breeze whispers

NOTES/THOUGHTS

WHICH WAY IS UP?

Why do birds sing songs after the rain?
When all I feel is deep sorrow and pain
Eternity comes and goes each day
For the good things in life I pray
Yet I don't know why they don't come easy for me like they do for some
And I wonder time and time again if the best is yet to come
Life is spinning round and round before me and I'm searching for a clue
Cause I don't know where to turn I don't know what to do to change my view

Chorus: Which way is up when I'm so down I can't see around me   (2x)

Why is life so unfair for most?
Some work hard while some just seem to coast
All good things come to those that wait
If that's true then where lies my fate?
Always try to the right thing but it doesn't come out right for me
Just a break for me Lord please I'm begging make my dreams reality
So I can help those who need help then help myself and help my family
Point me to the light so I might live forever after happily

Chorus: Which way is up when I'm so down I can't see around me   (2x)

Bridge: It's not the first time it won't be the last
The future seems darker than all of my past
Give me an inch cause I can't grab a mile
It might as well rain the next time that I smile

Chorus: Which way is up when I'm so down I can't see around me   (2x)

NOTES/THOUGHTS

SOME THOUGHTS FROM THE VAULT

VOL.1 NO.1 NEAL SELLERS
3/5/89
8:30 a.m.

As I look back, per chance it was fate
That I was able to seize the second chance to state
Some revelations about you, to you, through you
From a distance I studied, admired from afar
In the darkness that surrounds me, yet your soul breeds light
Yet I know not you, yet I think I do
The image is savage, bold, deceptive, contrite
My thoughts are pure at the moment, yeah right!
Brains, beauty, body send a bolt through those that can't handle your womaness
You search to find someone who commands, yet understands life, light, and love
For to understand life, you must live it
To understand light, you must dim it
And to understand love, you must feel it...

NOTES/THOUGHTS

VERBAL GYMNASTICS

Woooo, Mic's a blazin'
My verbal épée proves that God is amazin'
Armed with the Weapons, my rhymes could be an elegy
A friend of me once said, "Que's a walking dictionary"
Who be ye who steps to challenge me?
Get placed under earth because of your iniquity
I terror foes in this game for marmalade
For uncircumcised MC's, I'm the rusty blade
I will destroy the beasts thereof
Because the King of my castle no one is above
The Sexual Intellectual is the mixer
For honeys whose G-spot needs an elixir
Warning! To keep me off that behind?
Don't ever let me step inside of your mind
My verbal stimulation brings mental intoxication
The physical interpretation is orgasmic sensations

NOTES/THOUGHTS

HEAR YE... HEAR YE...
(Senryu)

NEAL SELLERS
8/13/23
9:08 p.m.

hate not the person
that brings the bad news to you
but the fact there is

NOTES/THOUGHTS

FIRE

I've got this joy... I just can't explain
I just can't contain... I just can't remain... Silent naw (no)...
Glory be his name... my life is not the same
He washes away stains... his life was not in vain (to me)
He takes away my pain... he keeps me in my lane
I'll forever praise his name... cause

Chorus: He's like fire... shut up in my bones
Shut up in my bones I said   (2x)
Shut up in my bones... Cause...

This is my testimony... confess sins... trust him totally
He's comfort when you're lonely... he died for our sins solely
Your love is for him only... in holy matrimony...
we don't deserve his glory
I will keep sharing his story... cause

Chorus: He's like fire... shut up in my bones
Shut up in my bones I said   (2x)
Shut up in my bones... Cause...

Bridge: (Wooo) God is love
I feel his love   (2x)
I need his love
I want his love (I'm say it again)

I'm not alone... if he's been good to ya
Saints sing hallelujah... step into your future
Give praises due
His grace is everlasting... his blessings for the asking... your soul feels satisfaction
You better praise him
Get up on your feet... get up out your seat right now... hands up in the air... cause

Finale: He's like fire... shut up in my bones
Shut up in my bones I said   (2x)
Shut up in my bones... Cause...

NOTES/THOUGHTS

SEA OF CHAFF

NEAL SELLERS
5/16/23
4:41 p.m.

Where is the wheat in this sea of chaff?
I mull this discomfort confined in a raft
A continuous paddle to the unknown I travel
In search of my destiny before I unravel
'Tis endless the chaff I see beyond reach
Yet steady my course is, for the wheat I beseech
Pondering what, when, who, where, why do I persist?
There is purpose within me, therefore 'tis hard to resist
A drive to believe that I shall achieve
Propels me on this journey, to wit... the will to succeed

NOTES/THOUGHTS

...AND YOU DON'T STOP

...A blast from the past and it's coming full circle
Neal Sellers is the name and the name is universal
Went to the University of Rochester
Pledged Que Psi in the second semester year of 85, my sands? I got five
'Cause I step to a groove, my dog tag is 2 Smooth
Anyway in 87 got my college degree
Finished law school in two years at Hofstra University
But if you look back upon my life story
You'd be shaking your head hearing this little testimony...

NOTES/THOUGHTS

NATURE'S NEMESIS
(Haiku)

NEAL SELLERS
8/2/23
3:52 p.m.

man shows no regard
for the splendor of nature
he seeks dominion

NOTES/THOUGHTS

YOU GOT TO GO

When will it stop? Oh where do I draw the line?
I got this feeling that I'm not the only one on your mind
You turn your phone down lying that the beeps are alerts
But all the games that you play someone's 'bout to get hurt
You got me all in my feelings with your "I love you so's"
You keep me crying with my girls yelling "Mo he got to go"
You got me vexed spending my checks on these hookers and hoes
You 'bout to have me digging holes in places nobody goes

Chorus: You got to go
Why you stress me acting like you don't know
You got to go
I'm about to usher you to the door
You got to go
Why you stress me acting like you don't know
You got to go
I'm about to usher you to the door

You were my biggest cheerleader when I got my new man
So why you all in his face talking like you trying to smash?
'Pose to be my best friend why you crossing the line?
Pushing up on mine? Chick I'm 'bout to beat your behind

Chorus: You got to go
Why you stress me acting like you don't know
You got to go
I'm about to usher you to the door
You got to go
Why you stress me acting like you don't know
You got to go
I'm about to usher you to the door

Bridge: Don't be afraid to be in love with yourself
Show off your self-worth don't undermine your virtue
Cause respect is not earned (ladies) respect is a given
And if you're not being treated the way you want to be treated
Look 'em dead in the eye and make damn sure you repeat it (ladies)

NOTES/THOUGHTS

Chorus: You got to go
      Why you stress me actin' like you don't know
      You got to go
      I'm about to usher you to the door
      You got to go
      Why you stress me actin' like you don't know
      You got to go
      I'm about to usher you to the door

NOTES/THOUGHTS

THE GROWTH OF THOUGHT

NEAL SELLERS
7/10/23
1:53 p.m.

I can...
I will...
I did...

NOTES/THOUGHTS

WE CAME HERE TO PARTY (THAT'S WHAT'S UP) FREESTYLE

...Take me away cause I plead guilty to the ultimate crime
Sometimes I'd rather skip the boots and just massage your mind
But if your mind is in a state in which you cannot relate
I'll have your body talkin' to me, yo, and make no mistake
'Cause I can revive, ya don't believe me, ask her then
It took seven whole days to make Toni Braxton breathe again...
The Sexual Intellectual does not mack
I deliver what you lack on a Facebook chat...

NOTES/THOUGHTS

DEPTH OF PERCEPTION
(Senryu)

NEAL SELLERS
7/26/23
10:25 a.m.

imagination
expressing minimally
life is my haiku

NOTES/THOUGHTS

I JUST WANT TO BE YOUR FRIEND

You don't trust a soul, and now you're cold and distant like a rolling stone
There's no comfort zone, cause baby let me tell you I've been there before
You want to be alone, I said the same thing too, but if I'd only known
To pick up the phone, I'd have save myself some misery
But all you need to know is...

Chorus: I just want to be your friend (4x)

Time marches on, you haven't changed one bit and I've expected that
But as a matter of fact, I'm there for you, cause I know what you're going through
I'll be your sounding board, I'll be the sacrificial lamb to heed your verbal sword
And still I pray the Lord, will help me heal your wounded heart
But all you need to know is...

Chorus: I just want to be your friend (4x)

It's now judgment day, you've come upon the crossroads and you need to know
Whether to let me in, I was there in the beginning and I'll see the end
Your heart won't let you bend, your mind is playing tricks on you and
Yet you tend to want to be my friend, you ask me why I'm doing this
But all you need to know is...

Chorus: I just want to be your friend (4x)

Bridge: Take my hand and I will lead you through the storm and the rain
Take my hand and we can conquer all your fears and your pain
Take my hand and all you stand to do is prosper and gain
Take my hand, you'll never be the same...

But all you need to know is...

Finale: I just want to be your friend

NOTES/THOUGHTS

THE NATURE OF HUMANITY

NEAL SELLERS
3/9/23
6:47 a.m.

Woman. Loving and nurturing. Complex, yet simple
Man. Protective and providing. Seeking, yet unfulfilled
Together. Harmonious and divided. Repellent, yet attractive
Hate. Destructive and evil. Wrong, yet easy
Love. Godly and fulfilling. Right, yet hard...

NOTES/THOUGHTS

LIFE OF A PLAYBOY

It's the life that I lead... full of fun and pleasure
Meeting someone new no matter where I go
My raps are never ending... that you cannot measure
I get smiles and sighs and all the ladies know
About my reputation all over the nation
And the talk around town about my love sensation
The main attraction... the ladies satisfaction
A lot less talk and a whole lot of action
You'll want to say no but your body will overrule you, yes!
You lost control... wake up alone before you can guess
That you're a nominal asset in my world of fun
The life of a Playboy is seldom done...

NOTES/THOUGHTS

SHE BE THE BADDEST...
(Senryu)

NEAL SELLERS
8/21/23
8:12 p.m.

lyte as a boulder
lyrical flow crush your soul
so what's your status?

NOTES/THOUGHTS

MAKE ME LOVE YOU AGAIN

Do you want us to work?
Is there love in your heart to make me love you again?
Can this be a new start?
Will you mend the heart you've broken, heal the pain
You need to...

    Chorus: Make me love you again
    (Because I'm broken)
    Make me love you again
    (Yet still I'm hoping)
    Make me love you again
    (My love is open)
    Make me love you again

Are you willing to work?
I'm not the same naïve girl that you told lies I believed
Can I bury your past?
Make me see you have changed, that there's a future for us
You need to...

    Chorus: Make me love you again
    (Because I'm broken)
    Make me love you again
    (Yet still I'm hoping)
    Make me love you again
    (My love is open)
    Make me love you again

    Bridge: You've got to prove your love to me
    There's no in between
    You're either in it for real
    Or you're not playing for keeps
    If you're not sincere, leave
    But if your choice is to stay
    Love will be what you make it
    But here's what I know
    You need to...

NOTES/THOUGHTS

Chorus: Make me love you again
         (Because I'm broken)
         Make me love you again
         (Yet still I'm hoping)
         Make me love you again
         (My love is open)
         Make me love you again

Finale: Make me love you again

NOTES/THOUGHTS

CHINA DOLL

NEAL SELLERS
10/17/96
9:32 a.m.

Her exterior... hard, but her features are soft, yet exquisite
Her shape challenges the many laws of physics
She possesses the rare combination of what I call the 3 B's
That's brains, beauty, and body for all those who know not what I mean
Her eyes sparkle as a diamond should (God Bless those eyes!)
But she's my China Doll, and it's unlikely that anyone else's could
Her smile is flirtatious, her eyes are contagious
Her stages of beauty are in a word, vivacious
She's beauty in anger, she's beauty in sadness
She's beauty in things that really don't matter
Inside my China Doll are the finest ingredients known to man
However, her beauty has been tarnished from the negligence of other hands
Hands that have not cared as my hands have fared
Hands that provide the touch where no one else's can compare
I do not worship my China Doll, but genuine is the love for her
Yes... I can take her off my mantel and replace her with another
But another would not be her, for she is truly unique
And what makes her extra special is my China Doll actually speaks
She speaks of communication and men have rarely listened
She saw that I did and my China Doll allowed herself to glisten
For a moment she allowed me to mold her, to hold her, to comfort and console her
But now her "lack of love" for the letter "V" has threatened her being "in love" with me
Her desire not to hurt him has caused her to sacrifice her true lover, incredibly
In her world of choices I wonder how I became her casualty
When in actuality, her beauty and my beauty made our reality
Am I dreaming or has the temperature on my China Doll gotten colder?
Am I the love of her life or just a needy shoulder?

NOTES/THOUGHTS

LIFE FINDS A WAY
(Haiku)

NEAL SELLERS
8/2/23
5:08 p.m.

the ecosystem
bows to the will of nature
man has no say so

NOTES/THOUGHTS

THE INSANITY THAT WE CALL LOVE

This thing called love... I play cool... it takes over me
It's gloom... it's glee... it hurts like a sting from a honey bee
But I like it... this insanity that we call love

This thing called love... I want... inside of me
It's friend... it's foe... it hurts like frostbite on my toes
But I like it... this insanity that we call love

Magnifique... très chic... ooo wee... found me a dishy lady
We wine... we dine... wait what... she's winning over me
I can't fight it... this unrelenting thing called love

I love... I cry... I hate... I can't handle it
Please God... restore... my faith... in humanity
Cause I'm hurting... from the insanity of losing love (of his daughters)
The insanity of losing love (of his daughters)
The insanity that we call love

(But) he dreams... he tries... those eyes... he can have all of this
I see... the flaws... in awe... that I still commit
Got me buggin'... the insanity that we call love

I freeze... tongue's tied... I stumble over words I've known all my life
She's wild... runs free... when I tame Black Beauty... I'm a saddle free Bronco buster
For this insanity that we call love

Chorus: The insanity that we call love (3x)

Bridge: In time... I see... the change in how he acts toward me
He can't... deflect... the anger that he feels within
We yell... we scream... we suffer in once was a dream
But then... within... a feeling so strong I just can't explain
It's not normal... this insanity that we call love

Despise... those eyes... the way they look through me yet I can't deny
(All) the love... that I feel... confliction that may haunt me til the death of me...
But I love him... the insanity that we call love

NOTES/THOUGHTS

In time... love finds... a way... when you open up your heart
Love is God... God is love... you will find... at the end of this maze as you brave through
The insanity that we call love

Finale: The insanity that we call love

NOTES/THOUGHTS

A TASTE FOR SWEETNESS

NEAL SELLERS
1/21/95
9:34 a.m.

I have a sweet tooth and it's really misbehavin'
The more I think about it, the more I'm cravin'
So for breakfast this morning, I'll partake on doughnuts
No jelly, no cream please, just milk... yes, two cups
Lunch time already, oh my how time flies!
But I've got to have my sweet potato pie
Well, what do you know, it's two-thirty, time for snack
A friend suggests Snickers... but I'm feelin' a KitKat!
Seven o'clock... dinner time! Do I unwind with wine?
Nope! A tantalizing chocolate cream puff will do just fine
You would think after that I would have no room for dessert
But look who's made pudding, a few bowls wouldn't hurt!
Sweetness is my weakness... natural, raw, unrefined and pure
Is honey the remedy? Maybe, for baby bear... but for Papa Bear's addiction,
Your hot chocolate is the cure!

NOTES/THOUGHTS

SEED OF DESTRUCTION
(Senryu)

VOL. 1 NO. 31   NEAL SELLERS
                                             8/12/23
                                             9:50 a.m.

       dismal surroundings
     that's what the world is today
          realm of confusion

NOTES/THOUGHTS

CAPTURE THE RHYTHM

Capture the rhythm get caught in the flow
Make sure you can feel it before you let go
When others forsake you and cause you despair
Take comfort in knowing God is always there (Shift gears)

Back to the rhythm where the only decision is a mission
To rush the dancefloor... no indecision
And I'm giving just what you asked for
Peace and harmony co-exist because we cast off
Racial division... it's the vision
To make all ye stand united
You're invited... get excited
Don't fight it... enlighten...Mmmm... as we

Chorus: Capture the rhythm and don't let it go
Take hold of the rhythm and let yourself go (2x)

Live-your-life with faith hope and charity
Have compassion seek wisdom seek clarity
Love your neighbor in all that you do
Forgive all transgressions as God forgave you (Repeat verse)

Live-your-life with faith hope and charity
Have compassion seek wisdom seek clarity
Love your neighbor in all that you do
Forgive all transgressions as God forgave you (Umph shift gears)

Circle up the wagon don't sweat the reaction
As we take you on a journey bringing pure satisfaction
Then 1,2,3 hop... 1,2,3 hop
Turn to the middle give your shoulders a wiggle
Don't let the fun ever fizzle... keep the party on sizzle
And then stop... jiggle your end game... stop... jiggle your end game

Chorus: Capture the rhythm and don't let it go
Take hold of the rhythm and let yourself go (2x)

NOTES/THOUGHTS

Bridge: I want hands up in the air... I want hands up in the air (2x)
          (Then simultaneously)
          Throw your hands in the air
          (Crowd response)
          Cause we don't care (4x)

Bridge 2: Take it down, bring it up, take it 'round the world and don't stop (4x)

                Finale: Join the movement (Repeat)

NOTES/THOUGHTS

COMMUNITY ACTIVIST

NEAL SELLERS
7/14/13
5:26 p.m.

So you say in light of the Trayvon Martin decision
What can I do to make a difference going forward?
I'm glad you asked
For starters, you can
MAKE THE TIME to get involved in your own community
Get more informed about local politics
When there is a community meeting... attend
Local ordinances that affect your area are discussed
When there is a school board meeting... attend
School programs are born and die there
When your city or state rep has an open house... attend
You can find out what future laws are being proposed
And how they affect you BEFORE they become law
And if those same reps do not have those dialogues?
Demand that they do
Change cannot be effectuated without a voice for it
Support community leaders, become community leaders
Get to know them and hold them accountable
So they can hold others accountable...
Learn how to organize and use local boycotts for change
Then it is easier to move up the ladder, city, state, and national
Vote... get someone else registered so they can vote too!
Take jury duty seriously
Send that form back and show up when called
While you may not be selected
There is strength in numbers
Meaning the more that show up
The more that have to be pre-emptorially challenged
I don't even want to think about the people that may have ignored their jury notice
Perhaps opening the door to one of the persons on that Trayvon Martin jury
Need I remind you justice could very well depend on it...

NOTES/THOUGHTS

POETRY IN MOTION
(THE GIFT OF GAB)

...In '92 here's what we're gonna do (4x)
We're gonna rock the nation, every radio station
And maybe get some standing ovations
Smell the Lagerfeld cologne from my body
Enough to catch a young fan club of hotties
Peace to Reese, better known as Mix Master Ice
And nuff shouts go out to the DJ Dice
I wanna send out thanks to the man above
For letting David Neal Sellers do what he loves
Chose music over law so I could go "Yes Y'all"
Plan to have my own label by the fall
There's only one more thing, Yo I'm not foolin'
Tell Eddie, I'm after Whitney Houston...

NOTES/THOUGHTS

NIGHT OWL
(Haiku)

NEAL SELLERS
8/4/23
8:20 a.m.

the stillness of night
a time for wisdom in thought
to be a night owl

NOTES/THOUGHTS

WE CAME HERE TO PARTY
(THAT'S WHAT'S UP)

We came here to party baby... where those red cups?
Yo why is everybody sittin'? Get yo ass up!
We came here to party... no one's playin' the wall
No one's sittin' down until the bar says "Last call"

Chorus: We came to par-ty... people... yeah that's what's up
We came to par-ty... people... yeah that's what's up
Let's get this par-ty... people... now that's what's up
Let's get this par-ty... people... now that's what's up

We came to drop knots in this spot
So keep the ruckus with you
But if you bring it
Know that we can bring them things in here too
But we not tryin' to go there
We'd rather stay here with you
And party up with bottles... models... and the 'round the way crew

Chorus: We came to par-ty... people... yeah that's what's up
We came to par-ty... people... yeah that's what's up
Let's get this par-ty... people... now that's what's up
Let's get this par-ty... people... now that's what's up

We came here to party baby girl that's what's up
So turn that body 'round then park it... yeah that's what's up
We came here to party baby girl that's what's up
Drinks up in the air... now drop it... yeah that's what's up

Chorus: We came to par-ty... people... yeah that's what's up
We came to par-ty... people... yeah that's what's up
Let's get this par-ty... people... now that's what's up
Let's get this par-ty... people... now that's what's up

NOTES/THOUGHTS

PLIGHT OF A WRITER

NEAL SELLERS
3/14/23
11:17 p.m.

The words stir within me, hoping for their opportunity to meet my neighbor, paper
But is it good enough for the world? That is my labor
I wake up in the middle of the night with inspiration to write
So I jot down lines without insight
Some lines tease with anticipation to enlight
In other lines I see wit, enough to leave as first written, and I just might
I ponder clarity, I ponder hidden meanings
I ponder if I like it after many many readings
I decide that I do, but will the public like it too?
The plight of a writer, and ultimately I decide
I don't care if they do...

NOTES/THOUGHTS

FEEL THE HEAT/ BROOKLYN FREESTYLE

DJ Dice Brooklyn bringing danger to mankind
I'm 'bout to blow up because this world is my land mine
The gold medal letterer dot dot dot et cetera
The Apex Predator stepping on any competitor
I'm sipping Uncle Nearest and my stogie is lit
I ran up in these streets with Kiki, Ian and Fritz
Breukelen, Brevoort, Pink Houses, South Shore
I've even ducked shots at Lucky's Corner Store
My flow tastes of water, simple and plain
Like life's liquid nourishment, I'm too complex to explain
Thinkin' 'bout steppin' to me? I would defer
The end is you... You are no more... You were
I pledge allegiance to the borough of Brooklyn
I take exception to your bark if you're not friend
I say whatever is clever and never ever caught in inclement weather
90's massive forever (Boh! Boh!)
Heed the spoken word, my tongue is just the vessel
To speak God's truth many years I've had to wrestle
Neal Sellers authored "The Cackling of the Crows"
The paradox as such comes off as ineffectual
To be continued... Bless up... The Sexual Intellectual

NOTES/THOUGHTS

HALF MAN... HALF AMAZING
(Senryu)

NEAL SELLERS
8/19/23
6:50 p.m.

arrogant i am
yet i am also humble
a dichotomy

NOTES/THOUGHTS

SONNIE DAYS

NEAL SELLERS
10/17/96
8:40 a.m.

My life has seen sonnie days
But today it's cloudy, and I'd rather not have it this way
How ironic, it looks like it's going to rain outside
But my heart tells me it's already pouring inside
Drops of water have hit the page, as outside and inside
Meet to turn my sonnie days to grey
I could write a novel telling you about my sonnie days
But suffice it to say, her eyes were the window to my soul, okay?
On sonnie days, the rays are narcotic, the eyes feisty, yet bright
On sonnie days, the rays could be steamy, just right for a passionate night
On sonnie days, I remember tubs, backrubs, and a musically filled birthday
On sonnie days, I remember my China Doll, special numbers and secret hideaways
When I think of sonnie days, I think of all the joy that was
And get angry at all the joy that could and should be
But alas, understanding has been my forte... splendid!
But I'll be damned if I can put an "H" on my chest and handle it!
The forecast? Sonnie skies? I wish I could say
But for now, all I can hold onto is yesterday... and yesterday is my tomorrow, today
In the eye of the storm within your heart
Find your peace and know whom thou art
But also know that spiritually, emotionally, mentally, and physically
No one will ever come closer than I in fulfilling your ecstasy or fantasy, yes indeed!
My life has seen sonnie days
And I'd rather not have it any other way

NOTES/THOUGHTS

GOD ALMIGHTY
(Haiku)

NEAL SELLERS
9/1/23
12:45 p.m.

honored by your grace
you are awe inspiring
i am not worthy

NOTES/THOUGHTS

PARTY PEOPLE

Chorus: Party people   Get it poppin'
               My party people   Let's get this poppin' off
               Party people here   Let's get it poppin'
               My party people here   Let's get this poppin' off

Verse: How do you want me?   Baby boy
               Tell me how you want me?   Baby boy
               From the front, from the back
               If you choose, you can't lose
               How do you want me?   Baby boy

               How do you want me?   Baby boy
               Tell me how you want me?   Baby boy
               Though your lips haven't moved
               Your eyes, they stay glued
               How do you want me?   Baby boy

Chorus: Party people   Get it poppin'
               My party people   Let's get this poppin' off
               Party people here   Let's get it poppin'
               My party people here   Let's get this poppin' off

Verse: We came here to party   That's what's up
               So what you wanna do?   That's what's up
               If you don't know what's next
               I suggest that you step
               Step off the dance floor   That's what's up
               Cause when my crew come through
               Make sure the ones and twos
               Just keep spinning hot sounds
               D.J. hold it down, let's make it happen   That's what's up

Chorus: Party people   Get it poppin'
               My party people   Let's get this poppin' off
               Party people here   Let's get it poppin'
               My party people here   Let's get this poppin' off

NOTES/THOUGHTS

Bridge:	Party over here	
	The party's over here (3x)	(2x)
Chorus:	Party people	Get it poppin'
	My party people	Let's get this poppin' off
	Party people here	Let's get it poppin'
	My party people here	Let's get this poppin' off

NOTES/THOUGHTS

BLISS

NEAL SELLERS
7/14/23
5:30 p.m.

The backyard is the beginning
The sun hits my face and I cannot help to think that I am winning
I unfurl the umbrella and the covering is complete
I take in the moment and then I take a seat
I pick up a stogie and take a whiff
The aroma is intoxicating, the stick is stiff
The wooden match is eager to ignite with a kiss
The cigar is lit. I take a puff... bliss

NOTES/THOUGHTS

REJUVENATING
(Senryu)

NEAL SELLERS
9/22/23
7:07 a.m.

let down your hair from
the insecurities of
life and choose to bloom

NOTES/THOUGHTS

SOUL TO BODY

Dianetics is the science of the mind
I'ma break it down in this rhyme
Relax your mind you hear the beat... sweet
I hear tapping... look at your feet
Now you get up and dance and people whisper it's true
Slide side to side... Hammer can't touch u
See the urge was there down in your soul
Then your body rebelled your mind lost control
It's destined to be and ya see that's the key
Soul to body + me equals clear mentality

NOTES/THOUGHTS

A DIAMOND REBORN

NEAL SELLERS
3/8/95
7:27 a.m.

Can someone please explain this to me? I mean, I'm really quite perturbed
Yet at the same time I'm jumping for joy, which makes my prior thought seem absurd
You see, I stumbled upon a diamond recently, priceless in worth
Others have walked this path before, yet this diamond remained unearthed
"How can this be?" your thoughts echo to me,
"When this diamond is there for all to see!"
Well, let me explain to you how this diamond came to be
This diamond lacked luster, it was covered with dirt and grime
Because those that came into possession never really took the time
To remove the insecurities that make a diamond like this shine
Now you may be asking of yourself, "Self, how does a diamond have insecurities?"
Well you would have insecurities if you were surrounded by impurities!
A diamond comes alive when it is appreciated by light
A diamond does not sparkle when its' sunny days turn to night
A diamond craves affection... a lot... a little... even slight
A diamond which receives a lack of care will never shine as bright!
If no one takes the time to polish the surface
The beauty underneath just becomes worthless!
Thus when I began to rub the diamond and bathe it with my light,
I didn't know I would unleash
A spectacular spirit of life dimmed within the belly of her beast
With no visible flaws, the beauty emitted from this diamond was beyond imagination
And when my light caught it just the right way,
The beauty rivaled a setting of the sun correlation!
So that's why I'm perturbed, because I just can't understand
How such beauty could be lost at the hands of a man
But hey! Finders Keepers... Losers Weepers
Now that I have her, I'm damned sure gonna keep her!!!

NOTES/THOUGHTS

YOU BETTER LOVE ME

I'm tired of everyday Romeos
The lovers that swear they can hang
I wanna get lovin' all through the night
But what you bring to my tunnel should be more than light
If you let me I'ma take control move my body take your soul
If you let me I'ma grab a hold, take your load

Chorus: You better love me (4x)

I hope you don't mind me expressing
Just what I want you to do when you're undressing
Because if you can't saddle this properly
I'm gonna let the world know you couldn't handle me
If you let me I'ma set the rules can your tools fit these screws?
If you let me I'ma make you grin just don't bend

Chorus: You better love me (4x)

Bridge: Oooo ooo ooo nice and nasty that's the plan
         Oooo ooo ooo take me there if you're the man

I'm tired of everyday Romeos
The lovers that swear they can hang
I wanna get lovin' all through the night
But what you bring to my tunnel should be more than light
If you let me I'ma take control move my body take your soul
If you let me I'ma grab a hold, take your load

Chorus: You better love me (4x)

NOTES/THOUGHTS

PRIMITIVE UNDERSTANDINGS
(Haiku)

NEAL SELLERS
9/23/23
3:13 a.m.

a pungent odor
released in the wilderness
claims territory

NOTES/THOUGHTS

THE SANDS OF TIME

NEAL SELLERS
9/11/92
12:31 a.m.

Into the archives of time I wander
Do I write to impress thee... sometimes, I ponder?
To impress thee, impresses me
The point is reciprocal, that... 'tis the key
What do I see as I wander endlessly?
Our past and our future are destined to be
Lines, lines, my comfort is lines
Yet I'm confined by lines, 'cause my prison... is time
Time together... time apart
Time to rain and pour from the heart
Time is also something I dread
If I cannot face it with my... Mystic Red...

NOTES/THOUGHTS

GIRLS OF TODAY

...I was cooling on the campus of a State University
The brothers and the sweethearts of the best fraternity
Had turned a party out and with all sincerity
The others can't compete, we brought them back to reality
An after party moved us to a new domain
And in the early morning hours, we that did remain
Collaborated and debated issues using our brains
And all those that couldn't hang, we asked that they refrain
Because the talks were philosophical and made you think about
Life in new perspectives, things you don't see a shrink about
The topic changed to couples and the question was asked
If your woman went to work, could you handle the task?
That she was making more money than you had in the past
And if you wouldn't feel ashamed and walk around in a mask!?!
I didn't know about the others, but I knew how I felt
If my girl walked around with a big money belt
Well we'd Delancey, and Pitkin and 1-2-5
We'd hit the jewelry stores and baby I'd just buy buy buy
We'd hit the Av along Jamaica, then we'd stop for some tea
And if I felt like it, we'd probably stop by Fulton Flea...

NOTES/THOUGHTS

THE GUISE OF THE NIGHT...
(Senryu)

NEAL SELLERS
9/3/23
11:59 p.m.

the midnight hours
the playground of the devil
it's hot in these streets

NOTES/THOUGHTS

FOREVER AND A DAY

Winter has settled in and I'd like to let you know
That I've got a fire burning baby brought back from long ago
You bring out a passion that I've longed for you're the one friend that I need
You've reached me emotionally mentally spiritually sexually... yes indeed

Chorus: I'll love you forever... and a day (4x)

Spring is upon us and our love blooms like a rose
I think you're contagious cause I feel ya spread from my head down to my toes
When I'm with you I feel the world is mine and I hope you feel the same
And if we ever see cloudy skies... remember I can stand the rain

Chorus: I'll love you forever... and a day (4x)

Summer's a scorcher but yet I don't complain
Cause when the ice drips from your hand the pleasure's so insane
You feel like the wind feels on a muggy day I can never get enough
Like a river flowing endlessly through me... sho' nuff

Chorus: I'll love you forever... and a day (4x)

Fall has descended metamorphosis is strange
Because the leaves have turned colors but your beauty hasn't changed
I've crossed the rainbow to the other side and there I will remain
To come back over without you just wouldn't feel the same

Chorus: I'll love you forever... and a day (4x)

Bridge: I'll love you forever... You can count on me I'll always be there
I'll love you forever... A love like yours to have is something so rare
I'll love you forever... You're the treasure chest and I am the key
I'll love you forever... Definitely our love is destined to be...

Finale: I'll love you forever... and a day (8x)

NOTES/THOUGHTS

GAMBLING ON SURVIVAL

NEAL SELLERS
7/7/16
5:08 p.m.

So if I carry a gun illegally
I can get shot by the police
And if I carry legally and responsibly as the NRA suggests
Telling the police in plain ENGLISH I have a gun and a permit to carry
I can get shot by the police
So being a law abiding citizen has now turned into Russian Roulette
And I'm gambling with my life
Telling the people that are supposed to protect and serve me
That I can legally carry a firearm, and...
I can get shot by the police
Add this to the things a black man has to consider in America
And it is a shame a black man has to fathom this survivalist mentality in 2016
And I don't know a black man today
Who doesn't have a story about being pulled over, detained, or otherwise?
Growing up or even as an adult
That is a fraternity I am not happy to be in...

NOTES/THOUGHTS

RHYMIN' THE BLUES

...I went to the courts so I could vent a little frustration
Heck, if I had wanted, basketball could have been my occupation
Sure they were tall, but none of them had my skills
One of them made like Manute Bol and was swatting my stuff at will
I didn't like the fact that my man Ice had started laughing
So I began dazzling the crowd with my Magic Johnson passing
Behind the back here, then a blind pass I sent
The gold Benz was fresh... except for the brand new dent
Out of the car came Magic himself, the look in his eyes hurt
You know he took my Converse sneakers and then my autographed t-shirt!?!
But hell I wasn't angry, cause along came the crew
And right now we're just standing here, Rhymin' the Blues...

NOTES/THOUGHTS

SEDUCTION
(Senryu)

NEAL SELLERS
7/31/23
8:26 a.m.

aura is allure
sexual simplicity
never disappoints

NOTES/THOUGHTS

DON'T TAKE IT AWAY

Your exterior? Hard but your features are soft yet exquisite
Your body breaks laws of physics
You possess the combination of brains and beauty
What I'm sayin' is you're a definite cutie
Your smile is flirtatious, your eyes are contagious
Your stages of beauty are in a word vivacious
You're beauty in anger, you're beauty in sadness
You're beauty in things that really don't matter
Beep me with a code number to say you care
Others try to step to me but they don't even compare
How do I love thee let me count the ways
All I'm really sayin' is don't take it away...

Chorus: Don't ever take your love away
You always promised you would stay
Cause in my future all I see
Is that you will be here with me
Because of you December's May
Don't take your love away... don't take your love away

A spectacular spirit of life that's what you are
With no visible flaws that dimple's against the law
How such beauty found the hands of this man
I'll never ever truly even really understand
You're my diamond you're precious in worth
And I'll be by your side when it's time to give birth
When you hurt I hurt yes I feel your pain
And when things get sour I can stand the rain
Your sweetness is my weakness unrefined and pure
And for this addiction to you not even honey can cure
How do I love thee let me count the ways
All I'm really sayin' is don't take it away...

Chorus: Don't ever take your love away
You always promised you would stay
Cause in my future all I see
Is that you will be here with me

NOTES/THOUGHTS

Because of you December's May
Don't take your love away... don't take your love away

Follow me please to a place not far
Where the last few romantics gaze up at the stars
Eternal bliss? Or is it just happiness
When I smile... hmmph I reminisce
Tiskits and taskets that's all that I write
You're the first thing I see and the last thing at night
The darkness surrounds me yet your soul breeds light
My thoughts are pure at the moment... yeah right!
This place exists unlike Timbuktu
I call it paradise and my paradise is you
How do I love thee let me count the ways
All I'm really sayin' is don't take it away...

Chorus: Don't ever take your love away
You always promised you would stay
Cause in my future all I see
Is that you will be here with me
Because of you December's May
Don't take your love away... don't take your love away

No one knows me like you do
Who finishes my sentence who thinks for two?
I give my love and all my best
You got the key to my heart but wait here's the rest
With you I'm sincere when I say I'll be loyal
How I want to treat you a Queen couldn't feel this royal
If a picture could capture your likeness... it wouldn't
If a sunset could describe your radiance... it couldn't
And if a word could say how I feel it... it would... heh... but it couldn't
Check it... How do I love thee let me count the ways
All I'm really sayin' is don't take it away...

Finale: Don't ever take your love away
You always promised you would stay
Cause in my future all I see
Is that you will be here with me
Because of you December's May
Don't take your love away... don't take your love away

Chorus by Inaya Day

NOTES/THOUGHTS

WE

NEAL SELLERS
10/17/96
10:08 a.m.

If you could see yourself through my eyes you'd see two roses, one purple, one peach
...But I think you do!
If you could see yourself through my eyes you'd see the words of our love song
...But I think you do!
If you could see yourself through my eyes you'd see sonnie days, romantic nights and G Spot flights
...But I think you do!
If you could see yourself through my eyes you'd see that we belong together
...But I know you do!
...Then why aren't we?

NOTES/THOUGHTS

STREET LIFE FREESTYLE

Tic Toc (8x)
I punch the clock and spit bars for the masses
Monique Nikole is the sugar cane that yields molasses
Alas this street life is in us, ain't no classes
You learn how to move or else you fit a casket
It's drastic when you on the sidewalk in plastic
Cause thugs deem your street actions radioactive
Whether you hustle, walk the streets or 9-5
In Brooklyn, the goal is simple, stay alive
But just because you're alive doesn't mean you're livin'
So we take the big piece of chicken, that's a given
You looking at the best of both worlds combined
Street smarts, intelligence and your boy can rhyme
Raise a glass and toast whomever it is that suits ya
May the best of your past be the worst of your future
More life... more blessings... strive to be divine
Time to punch out, Monique Nikole its showtime

NOTES/THOUGHTS

PIT BULL IN A SKIRT...
(Senryu)

NEAL SELLERS
8/21/23
6:58 p.m.

she spits that hot fire
the smell of burnt egos wafts
eve of destruction

NOTES/THOUGHTS

KNOCK, KNOCK... IT'S LOVE

I knew a girl named Trudie
She was a friend in need
She brought her problem to me
A complex one indeed
She couldn't understand why love could hurt so bad
She couldn't understand how love could make you sad
When the time is right you'll know but for now girl ya should be glad
See a friend told me once in truth you can't miss what you never had
So go back home and wait patiently and in time you'll see
Words of wisdom girl at such a young age will mean nothing
'Til ya hear this phrase...

Chorus: Knock, Knock... it's love and I've come knockin' on your door my friend
If you're not at home I'll be back and answer all of your questions, then   (2x)

I knew a girl by the name of Candi
She got involved with married man, Randy
But along came a guy named Andy
And now he's complicated matters dandy
She couldn't understand why the road to love's not straight
She couldn't understand how the dice could determine her fate
Curiosity killed the cat but did you ever think the cat was smart?
In fact the cat would be alive today if it hadn't listened to its' heart
She said now what does that mean, I don't have a clue, so what's a girl to do?
Just take a four letter word like love x 2, it equals me and you
So go back home and wait patiently and in time you'll see
Words of wisdom girl at such a young age will mean nothing
'Til ya hear this phrase...

Chorus: Knock, Knock... it's love and I've come knockin' on your door my friend
If you're not at home I'll be back and answer all of your questions, then   (2x)

Bridge: The best way to understand love is not to understand love
you won't understand at all
Cause when you think you have it figured out you don't have it figured out
cause love leads into a brick wall

NOTES/THOUGHTS

Remember love comes knockin' and it keeps on knockin'
and it won't stop knockin' trust me
Because love don't care and it don't play fair lock your heart
cause love will steal the spare key

So go back home and wait patiently and in time you'll see
Words of wisdom girl at such a young age will mean nothing
'Til ya hear this phrase...

Finale: Knock, Knock... it's love and I've come knockin' on your door my friend
If you're not at home I'll be back and answer all of your questions, then

NOTES/THOUGHTS

A SWEET VIEW OF REALITY

NEAL SELLERS
1/21/95
8:32 a.m.

If a sunset could describe you, it would... but it couldn't
If a picture could capture your likeness, it would... but it couldn't
If chocolate could envelope your sweetness, it would... but it couldn't
And if a word could say how I feel, it would... but... it couldn't

NOTES/THOUGHTS

NADIA

...A foundation for love has been extinguished
It was harsh, but I've learned now to distinguish
True love versus a fantasy, friends versus transparency
Dreams it seems, not as effective when it's reality
Nadia, a young mind trapped inside a body
In retrospect, it's really melancholy
For me to perceive that she would trade me?
To get the booby prize, behind door #3, let's see
How did I love you, let me count the ways
I loved ya morning, noon, night of each and every day
I loved you more than life itself, I could have died for you
And at my tombstone site, it read, "What a fool!"...

NOTES/THOUGHTS

WHO WANTS TO BE KING?
(Senryu)

NEAL SELLERS
8/2/23
11:07 a.m.

heavy is the head
that does wear the crown because
life weighs the righteous

NOTES/THOUGHTS

2 SMOOTH (BLUES)

Walking down the street with a limp and a strut
You think you're kinda cute but you need to grow up
Try to get with me but I'm not the check to cash
With lines like Yo baby baby, please don't make me laugh
You can wear your pants off your butt if you please
If I show a little bit of this then I'm a tease
Why you wanna fake what you know you don't have?
You tell me 'bout a car yet you're seen in dollar cabs
Now you're getting paid and you wanna step to me
You call me lots of names when I don't accept your fee
Take some good advice and go learns your ABCs
Cause women aren't covered in your GED

Chorus: 2 Smooth... that's what you wanna be
But you're not the guy that's gonna get with me
2 Smooth... that's what you wanna be
But you're not the guy that's gonna get with me

Tell me that you love me but you can't settle down
I don't need commitment and I don't need you around
All we want is honesty but no you try to fake us
Then you get caught and you turn around and blame lust
Got a reputation as a lover so you claim
That when you're finished with me how I'll never be the same
Say you're all that plus a bag of potato chips
Ladies here we go again another stump with dead hips
Doctors, Lawyers, Dealers, and Exotic Male Dancers
Just to name a few who claim a women's prayers are answered
Yeah I know baby that could never be you
A lover like you could only be 2 Smooth

Chorus: 2 Smooth... that's what you wanna be
But you're not the guy that's gonna get with me
2 Smooth... that's what you wanna be
But you're not the guy that's gonna get with me

NOTES/THOUGHTS

Bridge: I once knew a smooth operator (Yeah)
        Said meet me on the G train (Yeahhhh)
        Our paths weren't the same, he must have took the plane
        Never met him, cause he already came
        I had to leave 'em... ya feelin' me?

Finale: 2 Smooth... that's what you wanna be
        But you're not the guy that's gonna get with me
        2 Smooth... that's what you wanna be
        But you're not the guy that's gonna get with me

NOTES/THOUGHTS

THIS PLACE I KNOW

NEAL SELLERS
9/4/92
10:35 a.m.

Follow me if you dare to a place not far
I've been there before, twinkle twinkle little star
But I traveled a different way before in search of the light
I remember it vaguely then, unlike now where it seems I just returned last night
Clams and bowling pins, an odd combination
But alas, we all need re-creation
Eternal bliss... or is it just happiness?
When I smile... I reminisce
Tiskits and taskets, that's all that I write
Oh to have your fruit, I'd cherish the bite
Of Adam and Eve I am not jealous
Because I too have been where many mortals relish
The place I speak exists, but unlike Timbuktu
That place is paradise and my paradise is you...

NOTES/THOUGHTS

CLAP CLAP CLAP

Should rap be left to weak minded Emcees that reek
That do not push the culture, but follow like sheep?
It's been a helluva ride but I'm thinking it's time to go... Clap clap clap!
Take it back to the time when folks listened for rhymes
And when double entendres encompassed the sound
We don't stop, we don't sleep, Brooklyn won't tolerate you clowns... Clap clap clap!

NOTES/THOUGHTS

THE SAND OF THE SEAS
(Haiku)

NEAL SELLERS
7/27/23
10:47 a.m.

even though finite
see the possibilities
of infinity

NOTES/THOUGHTS

YOU'LL NEVER WALK ALONE

In the darkness around me your soul breeds light
With you by my side there is life
There is love in our hearts... yet most know not love
When that light leads to love... look above

Chorus: For to understand life you must live life
And to understand light you must dim light
But to understand love you must feel what is love
It's when two become as one...
There'll be joy and disdain
There'll be passion and pain
But you'll never walk alone
You'll never walk alone

When I take my last breath
Through your tears know this
If you hold memories... life exists
So when you call... I am there
When you fall... I'm there
When you don't know your way... I am there

Chorus: For to understand life you must live through life
And to understand light you must dim light
But to understand love you must feel what is love
It's when two become as one...
There'll be joy and disdain
There'll be passion and pain

NOTES/THOUGHTS

Bridge: Through the years I pledge to thee
        You may walk in the rain
        Life may cause you some strains

Finale: But you'll never walk alone
        You'll never walk alone (3x)

NOTES/THOUGHTS

THE FAVORITE GIRLS
(Senryu)

NEAL SELLERS
7/31/23
2:32 p.m.

a hole in my heart
bleeds love incurably for
the favorite girls

www.ingramcontent.com/pod-product-compliance
Lightning Source LLC
Chambersburg PA
CBHW051703160426
43209CB00004B/999